Table of Contents

The English Springer Spaniel   5

The Dog for You?   11

English Springer Spaniels
   of the Past   14

Looks   18

A Note about Dogs   22

Glossary   23

Index   24

Further Reading/Website   24

The English springer spaniel is a popular companion for home and field.

The English Springer Spaniel

The English springer spaniel is a lively, handsome dog that is popular as a pet, show dog, and **gundog**. Springers are quick to learn and willing to obey.

ENGLISH SPRINGER SPANIEL FACTS

Weight: 40 – 50 pounds (18 – 22.5 kg)
Height: 19-20 inches (48-51 cm)
Country of Origin: England
Life Span: 12 – 14 years

The first springers were hunting dogs. Their name comes from one of their hunting skills. Springers were once known as springing spaniels. They make game birds "spring," or rush into flight.

Springers were hunting dogs before they became popular pets.

A springer retrieves a pheasant for its hunting buddy.

With their keen sense of smell, springers find hidden birds that a person cannot. A trained springer flushes a hiding bird only when its human companion gives the command. They also **retrieve** birds that a hunter shoots.

In the field, springers have great **endurance** and **agility.**

Springers have great endurance for field work.

An English springer spaniel fetches a rubber bumper during training.

A summer splash helps a springer cool off and burn energy.

The Dog for You?

The springer's many qualities have made it one of the most popular breeds in both the United States and Canada. Springers are playful, affectionate dogs. They love human attention, even from strangers.

They are also high-energy dogs. They need daily exercise, such as hunting, a long walk, **obedience** training, agility work, or another activity.

A pet springer does best if it lives in its owner's house but has plenty of room to romp outdoors.

Springers (shown here) are larger and leggier dogs than cocker spaniels.

English Springer Spaniels of the Past

Spaniels of many types have lived in Europe for at least 600 years. Only in recent years, however, has the springer been a "pure" **breed**.

In the 1800's, English spaniels were often named because of their size or color rather than by other features. Spaniels were called springers if they grew up to weigh over 25 pounds (11 kg). Dogs that may have come from the same litter, but that weighed less than the springers, were called cocker spaniels.

English springers and Welsh springers (shown here) are similar dogs with some of the same ancestors.

Springers wear thick double coats.

By the late 1800's, English spaniel **breeders** wanted "pure" springers. They began to select parent dogs more carefully.

In 1902, the Kennel Club of England recognized separate breeds – cockers and springers. The first "true" springers in the United States appeared in 1907.

Looks

English springer spaniels are medium-sized dogs with medium-length coats. The outer coat may be flat or wavy. The undercoat is thick and soft.

Show type springers (shown here) wear longer coats than the field type.

These field type springers wear two of the breed's common coat colors.

Springers raised for **conformation** show events tend to wear longer and thicker coats than springers raised for field trials.

Springer coats are a mix of white and a shade of either black or brown. Some springers are "tricolor" with white, black, and brown coats. Small freckles of color in springer coats are called "ticking."

This field springer's coat has black ticking.

Springer pups grow up to be medium-sized dogs of 40 to 50 pounds.

Springers have dark eyes and long, floppy ears. They have long legs and short, **docked** tails, like those of boxers or miniature schnauzers.

A Note about Dogs

Puppies are cute and cuddly, but only after serious thought should anybody buy one. Puppies, after all, grow up.

Remember: A dog will require more than love and patience. It will need healthy food, exercise, grooming, medical care, and a warm, safe place to live.

A dog can be your best friend, but you need to be its best friend, too.

Choosing what is the right breed for you requires homework. For more information about buying and owning a dog, contact the American Kennel Club or the Canadian Kennel Club.

Glossary

agility (uh JILL uh tee) – the ability to easily perform certain athletic tasks

breed (BREED) – a particular kind of domestic animal within a larger, closely related group, such as the English springer spaniel within the dog group

breeders (BREE duhrz) – those who keep adult dogs and raise their pups, especially those who do so regularly and with great care

conformation (kon for MAY shuhn) – the desired look and structure of a dog (or other animal)

docked (DOKT) – to have had a section of tail removed

endurance (en DUR ents) – the ability to continue an activity without becoming tired

gundog (GUHN dog) – any of the dog breeds used in hunting

obedience (oh BEE dee ents) – the willingness to obey; to follow direction or command

retrieve (ri TREEV) – to fetch

Index

agility   8, 12

American Kennel Club
22

birds   6, 8

coat   18, 19, 20

England   17

hunting   6, 12

Kennel Club of England
17

training   12

United States   11, 17

Further Reading

Carroll, David L. *The ASPCA Complete Guide to Pet Care*. Plume, 2001.
Ditto, Tanya B. *English Springer Spaniel*.
    Barron's Educational Series, 2005.
Furstinger, Nancy. *Springer Spaniels*. ABDO, 2006.

Website to Visit

American Kennel Club English springer spaniel page –
    http://www.akc.org/breeds/english_springer_spaniel/index.cfm
Canadian Kennel Club – http://www.ckc.ca
English Springer Spaniel Field Trial Association – http://www.essfta.org

About the Author

Lynn M. Stone is the author of more than 400 children's books. He is a talented natural history photographer as well. Lynn, a former teacher, travels worldwide to photograph wildlife in its natural habitat.